Discovering
Gwyn ap Nudd

No part of this publication may be reproduced, stored in a retrieval system, or transmitted in any form or by any means, electronic, mechanical, photocopying, recording, or otherwise, without written permission of the author.

© Vanda Lloyd 2018

Introduction
Chapter 1 - The Goddess
Chapter 2 – The God
Chapter 3 – Discovering Pan
Chapter 4 – Discovering Gwyn
Chapter 5 – Glastonbury Tor
Chapter 6 – Challenges
Chapter 7 – Looking and Questioning
Chapter 8 – Realisation
Chapter 9 - Gwyn ap Nudd in image and verse

Introduction

This book tells of my journey of discovery, walking and being called by Gwyn ap Nudd and his energies on 'The Isle' of Avalon, Glastonbury Tor. From my first journey when the Goddess called to me years ago and the challenges that brought to my more recent calling of the God, duality and exploration. Through walking the land that is the Isle of Avalon, also known as Glastonbury Tor, in all weather and seasons I tell of my feelings and findings through this physical and spiritual journey.

Featuring full colour photographic images, verse, and words this book will open up a world for you to see.

Come

Come follow

Come follow me

Come discover with me

See what I see

Chapter 1

The Goddess

The Goddess

What would you do, what did I do?

I trained for three years to become a Priestess of the Goddess on the land that is known as The Isle of Avalon. During and after that time for the next three years I also worked in ceremony, honouring, and connecting with the Goddess in her different guises. The Goddess I felt, held me, supported me and was with me at all times, through each waking moment of each day.

I walked the land; I have always walked though as often happens in my teenage years not enjoying it as much as I had as a child or when I became 'an adult'. I love walking, being out in nature, experiencing the elements, the sunshine, the rain, squelching along muddy footpaths and feeling the grass beneath my bare feet in the summer. When I say walking I don't mean the 'route march' walking, rather more I walk and then sit and then walk some more, sometimes not going far, maybe just around Glastonbury Tor, other times going further. I connected to Goddess in this way, feeling her in the air, the land, the seasons, walking and musing with ideas forming. I loved the Goddess and still do; though I must say I don't 'worship' her but 'honour' her.

The Goddess had called to me, not me to her; I first heard her name when standing on a bridge over a river in Derbyshire. It was a sunny day and the river flowed under the bridge, the sun catching the ripples making them look like 'natures diamonds' as I thought of them. While standing looking into the flowing water a name came into my thoughts but it wasn't a name I had ever heard before, it was Danu. It wasn't until several years later I found out who Danu was but the memory of hearing her name that day is still as vivid as it was then.

From then I started to discover paganism and the Goddess, realising that I had always 'been pagan' but never knowing it had a name. Circumstances changed in my life and what is called a significant life event blew my world apart. My whole world changed, nearly all I knew was taken away from me. Through this very painful journey she, I felt, held me and supported me, gave me a focus at all times, she was there for me and I called to her often. I needed to make changes and couldn't stay where I lived, so I chose to move counties, (not countries but it could have been the same thing for me).

I left behind my grown up family and chose to move to be nearer to friends I had made, the group I was involved with at that time, and experience a different lifestyle. Through circumstances at the time I was able to make these changes, redundancy was accepted and a freeing up of the 9 to 5 lifestyle evolved.

It wasn't easy; in fact it was more difficult that I had ever thought it would be. My retreat, my escape, had become my reality and I now had no retreat or escape. I missed my family and when I moved the town wasn't quite as I had expected it to be.

The people I knew were busy with their own lives, or they like I used to do, only visited for certain times of year. I lived in temporary accommodation for quite a few months, lovely accommodation and very friendly, it was like a gift staying in this accommodation, a break from the normal. I still had bills to pay but not the pressure of them, if that makes sense. I got to know a lot of people over the months staying there. However, I resisted getting my own place, I didn't want the commitment, it was too much at the time. Gradually though over the months I did start to settle and get used to living on 'The Isle' as some call it and eventually found my own place. I also found my new retreat, my escape, I would sit in the Chalice Well Gardens, walk on the land around the town, on the Avalon Marshes and further afield.

I started to take photographs and I write, turning my creativity into books, these included full colour images and writing or verse. Since then I have created walking books, verse books, stories and other books this way. I now spend each day walking, creating and producing. My earlier verse books are about my experiences of becoming and being a Priestess, the reasons for moving to 'The Isle' and my journey of change at that time.

It wasn't long after I had completed and dedicated as a Priestess of the Goddess/of Avalon that I started to wonder what the God was like.

Who was he?

Chapter 2

The God

The God

I read a couple of books about him and his aspects/guises but felt I didn't really know him and I couldn't get a sense of him from the books I had just read, I just didn't understand him at all. As things do I put the idea of exploring who he was to me further away and carried on with my life, being involved with the community, trying to make a living, meeting friends, and discovering this new way of life took up all of my time.

I had a brief relationship with a man during this time; it was three years after my husband had died and although I was nervous I felt I needed to give a relationship a chance again. So I said yes and started seeing this man. It turned out to be a short relationship, just two to three months really and although it didn't last long in time, to me it felt like it had lasted for years. The relationship came to an end which was quite a shock to me, as I hadn't seen it coming but 'oh my' did it 'trigger' a deep journey for me.

I started to look at my relationships with the significant males in my life and the situations I had been in. This took me to a very deep place and made me look inwards and also to the choices I had made. Through journeying with these feelings and the issues that came up, I gradually started to build up again a better understanding of me and my experiences and relationships with the male. My spirituality and my feelings for men had been challenged by the Goddess; she had opened up for me a place to look into. I could have chosen to do nothing but I choose to work with the issues that arose. It was a long hard, journey but eventually I came to a place where I was more comfortable with the male and myself.

Then the God resurfaced again!

Chapter 3

Discovering Pan

Discovering Pan

I knew that I still had no experience of the God at all and started to explore what this meant. I had briefly met a man to chat to and through talking to him I again wanted to explore what the God meant to me. I was drawn to go to some local woods, not too far from where I lived. I didn't really like woods, they always seemed dark on sunny days and wet on rainy days. I mostly chose to walk on open ground, on hills and footpaths with stretching views where I could sit and just be. But I was drawn to these woods, so off I went.

I found myself walking the footpaths through the trees, meandering in the lighter and darker places of the woodland, the heavily treed areas and the small glades, getting a feel of the woodland, what it smelt like, what it was like to walk in. I visited many times and started to sit and watch, feeling the earth I was sitting on, which was usually soft and mossy smelling of earth and leaves. Pine and tree smells floating in the air, the leaves and plants changing in smell as I walked along. Sometimes I would sit and watch the dance of sunshine filtering through the trees causing moving shadows on the ground or feel the rain dripping slowly through the trees and leaves until it reached the soft ground.

I sat and mused and meditated, sometimes for a short while, sometimes longer. I also wrote and took photographs on these visits; I slowly became more used to the woodland and I discovered that I liked it!

I would sit and gradually become aware of being 'absorbed' into the woodland, feeling the trees around me, hearing the birds sing and the distant sounds floating in the air. Seeing fleeting images through the trees, what was I seeing, a shape, a shadow, a movement, flicker of sunlight or something more? Images probably caused by the light and shadows, the shapes of trees and how they seemed to change as I sat and looked or were they? Sometimes seeing something out of the corner of my eye but when I turned to look it was gone.

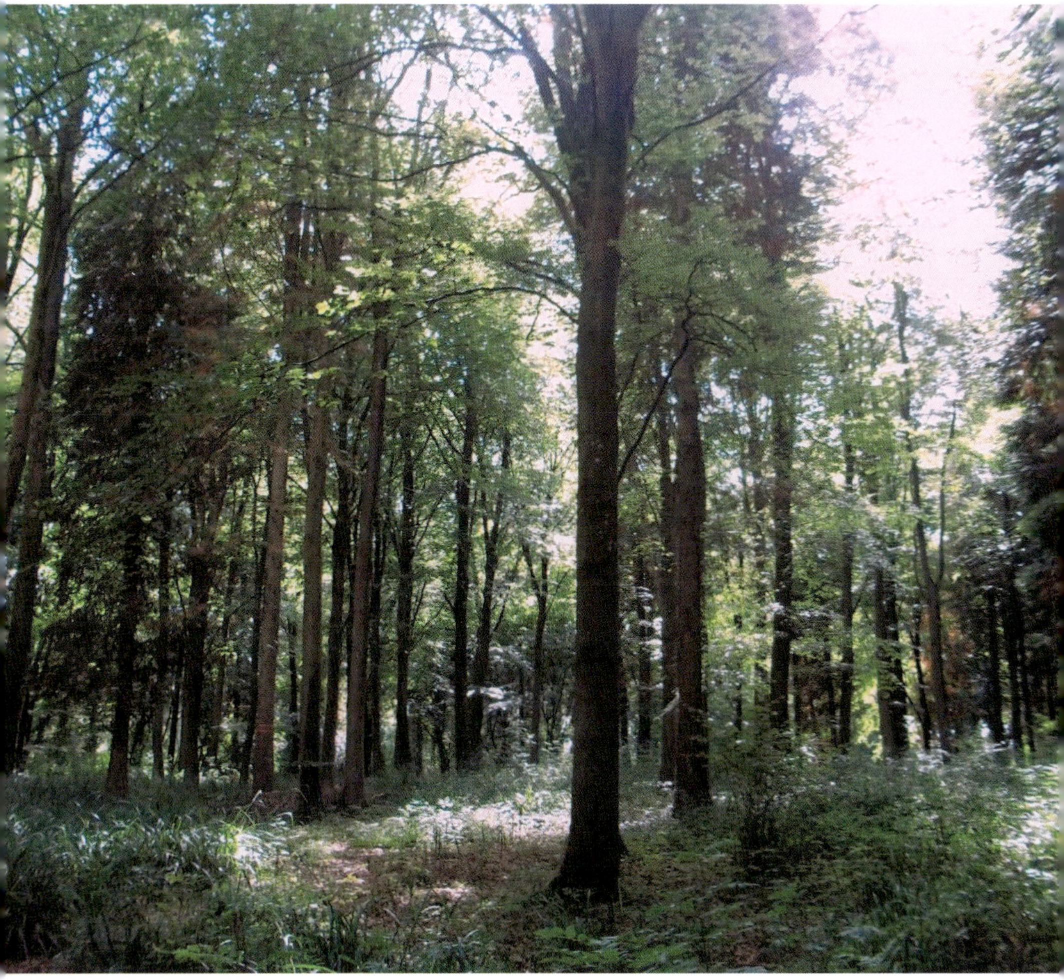

I started to become aware of a sense of Pan, the God. At this time I was still nervous of the male, of how the God may be, I was frightened of my own shadow and very unsure of what I may see or feel. I had read a little about Pan, the God of the Wild and I thought he would be rampant and a warrior.

Little did I realise that for me he would not appear in that way.

Over many visits, Pan appeared to me, so gently, so shy, hiding behind the trees in the woods, slowly and gradually emerging, knowing that I wouldn't have been comfortable if he had come in his 'wham bam' persona, I would literally have run away if he had done that. He gradually revealed himself to me through the shadows dancing on the sunlight days, dappled sunlight filtering through the woodland, showing me shadows and shapes until I realised who it was, who I was seeing and being so surprised at his gentleness. He would be the tree I could see out of the corner of my eye, the shape of a man or Pan, and sometimes he seemed to be holding a bunch of flowers! When I looked it was an actual tree, the shape of the tree against the others in the woodland did look like a man standing there but was it a tree or not?

Did the Lord of the Woodland come to me?
Shadowy shape within the trees
Was it him stepping without a sound?
No footstep marks upon the ground

Should I be wary of seeing him?
What is this realm that is beckoning me?
These shadowy shapes among the trees

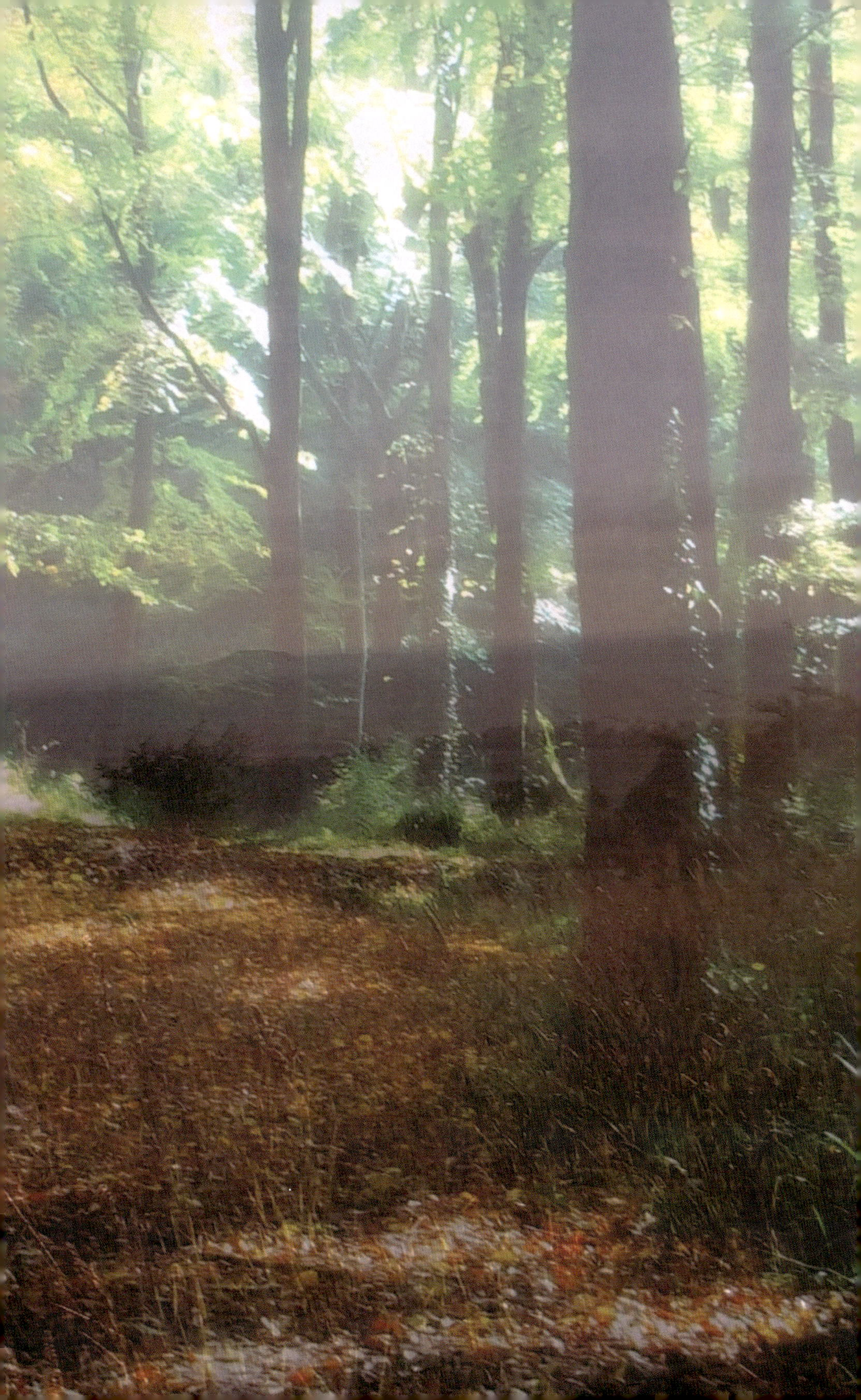

I wrote my words, my verses and took photographs to show Pan, how I saw him in the aspect that he emerged to me. I created gentle, shimmery images, between the worlds, the magic of illusion but of reality. The 'is he there or isn't he', glimpse and the belief that I know what I see. The words 'floating in verse' asking me to come explore the woodland footpaths, to explore this world and nature. I later came to create a book, The Woodland and The Fae, which tells in verse and image my story of his emergence.

I know Pan is seen in his guise of the rampant God with the nymphs and his sexual aspect very visible but he didn't appear to me like that. If he had I would have 'run a mile in the opposite direction'. If he had not appeared to me gently and shyly in his aspect of God of Nature and the Woodland I would not have been able to connect with him. My experience of the men I had deep relationships with up to this point created this reaction in me.

Interestingly I had been drawn to these woods by a man, a man who had created a bronze hare athame, one who put this hare in my hands to hold at a fayre he was attending and I had just happened to visit. I felt a deep sense of connection to the hare (and it emerged later, also with the man!). The hare brought to my mind the woods I had passed on a car journey and the ones which I eventually visited. After those first glimpses of Pan I visited the woods often, connecting more with Pan the God, he has always been gentle in his image to me. I became comfortable with the God in his guise of Pan, the Lord of the Woodland.

I was also now in a relationship with the man who had created the hare and from this relationship and walks with him on the land and in the woodland the idea of photographs and creating what would become The Spirit of the Woodland emerged. He was in a way representing Pan to me, playful, walks among the trees, being silly and hiding and playing seek, sitting in the meadow with the trees surrounding the edge, sunshine basking on our skin and me taking photographs of him in the heat and sunshine. He hiding among the trees leaves and branches, ferns and grasses around him.

I created images, at first in black and white, and then evolving to full colour of the male in nature, the male through the eyes of the female. These images featured a skyclad man, some images more 'full on' some subtle but always with the intention of showing the connection of man to nature and woman to man, especially in the woodland.

And then from some of these photographs I created collage images to show how I saw what was to me, the fleeting illusion of what could be Pan.

I produced the Spirit of the Woodland images and a calendar but what did surprise me were women's reactions to these images. Although there are many, many, images of naked women in all sorts of ways and positions and some very 'full on' ones at that, the feedback I was getting from my 'full frontal' images of the male was they weren't comfortable with this; they didn't want to see this really but wanted more subtle images, a suggestion rather than seeing all. I listened and changed the images, showing suggestion rather than full frontal view, though my intention had never been to feature and make prominent the male but rather the connection to the male and nature and how each complimented the other.

My relationship to Pan and the male continued and also with the Goddess. Now when I walked I sensed the Goddess and God, the duality rather than just one or the other.

She was equal to him
He was equal to her
They neither walked a step in front or behind
But together

'Spirit of the Woodland – Island Home'
The male in nature, seen through the eyes of the female

Chapter 4

Discovering Gwyn

Discovering Gwyn

Knowing and discovering Pan and working with him for quite a time I had a conversation with a friend just before Autumn Equinox 2016. We chatted about many things, the God being one of them. She is a very talented, gifted artist and wanted to have an exhibition with me. Me! Was I good enough?

I am a creature of sensitivity and always have my doubts! Her idea was for us to show Gwyn, Herne, Cernunnos, The Lords of the Hunt through image and verse. This idea of hers really did inspire and even before I would think could I do this images started to filter into my mind, glimpses of scenery and background and what I needed to do but................

Yes I was familiar with Pan but Gwyn! I knew hardly anything about, him apart from the fact that his name was connected with Glastonbury Tor. The thought of depicting him in an exhibition excited and frightened me at the same time.

Next day I found myself walking up Glastonbury Tor. As you do when you live in a place because 'it is there' you don't usually do it! So I hadn't been up the Tor for a long time. The other reason being that the last few visits had been quite panicky for me, bringing challenging thoughts to my mind so I had kept well away!

But there I was, on a beautiful September mid-morning the day before the autumn equinox, climbing to the top of the Tor, the images which floated into my mind needing to be photographed. I wanted background photographs but what to do with them I wasn't sure. I could 'see' atmosphere in my mind and lo and behold climbing up the Tor, there was the darkness and light, the sun and the cloud, the air blowing warmly and gently on this September day.

I 'captured' in photography what I had been seeing, the atmosphere, the broodiness, the fight of the seasons between the sunshine and the cloud.

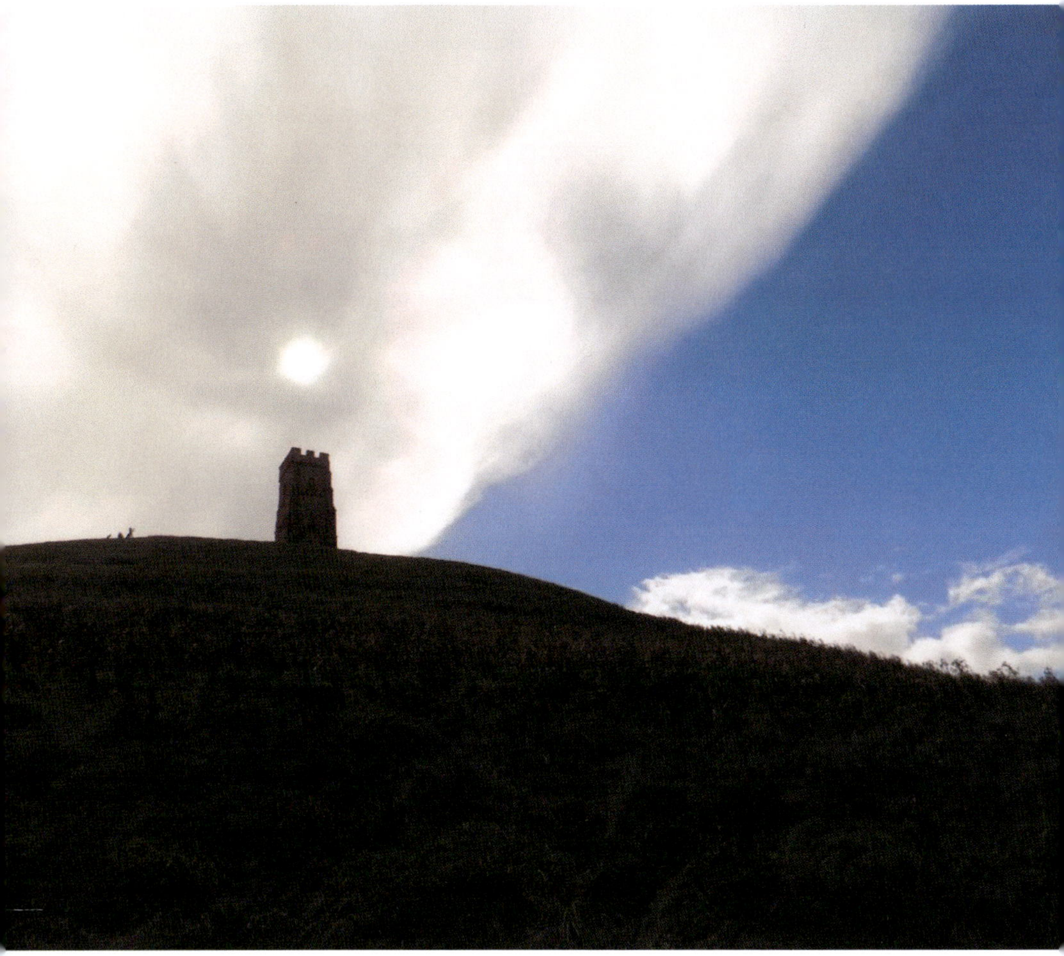

I sat on the land, on the ancient Tor, leaning against the Tower, sheltering from the wind that, although warm, was best in shelter watching the land below stretching out towards the sea. Seeing the greenness and beauty all around me, the blue sky and fluffy white clouds, the darker clouds gradually disappearing, for the fight of the seasons had been won by summer on this day. While I sat I asked Gwyn to show how he was to me, I knew little about him and while I could read books I wanted to discover who he is his through this way first, no informed opinion, no pre knowledge just to get to know him.

Words came, 'he was emerging again', around the Tor. Taking photographs I could sense something, the places I needed to photograph but no more than that. I still didn't know what he may look like to me.

Next day, Autumn Equinox, 22 September 2016, I found myself going to Chalice Well Gardens; it's free until 12 noon, so I needed to get there. A little out of breath, having rushed there after finishing a job, I got there just in time before the entrance charge applies again. I didn't mind paying that at all, it's just I didn't have the money and the Gardens were calling me to visit. Again like the day before, the sunshine and wind were warm. I always forget that the gardens will be busy when it's free to get in but that day it wasn't so bad, not too many people.

I sat by the waterfall and asked again for Gwyn to show me what I need to see, who is he?

The sunlight was filtering through the trees above the waterfall and I managed to capture in photographs the beauty of moss, tree and sunlight filtering through the leaves and I also found a new place to photograph the waterfall where the autumn sun filtered onto the water through the garden trees.

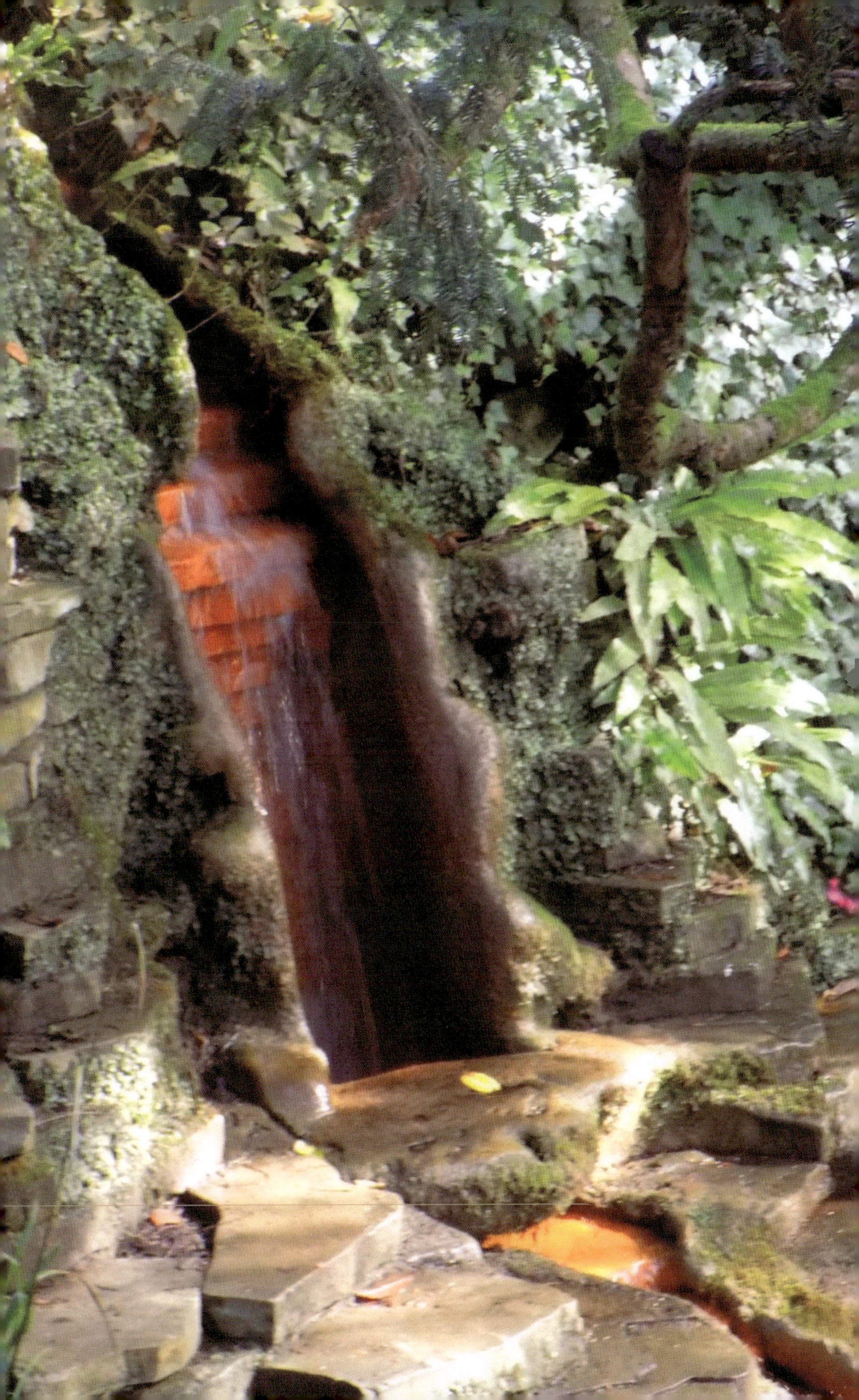

Then I walked into the meadow area becoming transfixed by the rowan trees, taking photographs of the abundant red berries. So much so that I sat on my little mat leaning against the gate by the rowan trees, the hot sunshine warming me against the cool breeze. I sat and mused..............

Gwyn, I look at the Tor from the Chalice meadow, Gwyn, who are you?

I sat for a while, musing, and thinking and just being. Feeling the pull of the Tor again, seeing it from where I sat. Then after a while and wandering round more of the gardens I left to walk on the Tor. Leaving Chalice Well Gardens and stopping briefly on the way at the White Spring. Seeing the gates which were painted red, white, and blue closed, meaning the White Spring as yet wasn't open, I made my way up the pathway to the Tor.

Walking the concrete pathway I followed the gravel path through the Fairfield and onto the bottom slopes of the Tor. Sitting awhile near the path, seeing Wearyall Hill in the distance and the colours of autumn leaves, browns and oranges and gold's all around me. I felt the pull towards the trees on the slopes of the Tor, not to the top of the hill itself so I walked to the woodland, the woodland, which is near to the eggstone, the entrance to the labyrinth. I walked a little way on the lower levels taking photographs, background photographs like the day before.

In my mind I am seeing Gwyn starting to gradually emerge and seemingly capturing this in my photographs, images come forming in my mind.

Seeing, as in this photograph, the glimpse of trees above the entrance stone, the blue sky and the very top of the tower.

But what does he look like, what does Gwyn look like? I muse as I walk along. All I can see at present are horns like stag horns, he has a sort of muscular physique but the image is so vague all I can see is the shape more than anything. He has white eyes but not just white, these seem more like white eyes with maybe black pupils.

Who is Gwyn, what does he mean to me
As I sit on the hill and look out towards the sea
The air is so warm in the equinox breeze
Sunshine and cloud as I sit at ease
Calling to Gwyn asking him to show how he is to me
As the view changes and I go to places he shows to me
What do I feel as I call to him
A sense of not yet knowing who he is
But knowing where to begin!

If only I could draw, I would then be able to capture what is there, fleetingly in my thoughts, but then my drawing isn't that good. Thinking, but I know I can write it, draw it through words, the images I am seeing and that is what I did. I sat writing the feelings that came to me, the thought of 'he is getting ready to emerge again'. All I 'saw' was a shadowy shape but I could feel his power within and under the land.

I was also walking, writing, and photographing my walks at this time for a book I was putting together and would eventually produce. So on this day and for that reason I decided to walk on Bushy Coombe. Not only to take photographs for my Walking book but also to get some photographs for the Gwyn images.

Or rather my intention was to go a walk up Bushy Coombe to get some more background photos. This I did but then found myself drawn towards the Tor! Again! I walked from Bushy Coombe, along the lane and into the field where the footpath would take me onto the other lane to the Tor. I love walking this way and through this field, it has the most amazing views over the levels if you look back and the Tor is there across the field. The view of the hill sideways on, showing some of the labyrinth levels especially when the sun is out and casts its shadow highlighting the levels. That day the sun was nearly overhead the tower on the very top with a lone figure standing on the hill.

Such amazing photos and a lone figure standing on the very top near to the tower, it wasn't Gwyn, I knew that, but it did remind me of the images that were starting to appear in my thoughts.

I then carried on walking to the bottom of the Tor, through Moneybox field and into the Avalon Orchard.

It was only after going through the Orchard and onto the bottom slopes of the Tor that I noticed the half moon, just like the sun appearing nearly over the Tor. I took some photos; I was blown away by the fact that not only had I managed to get the sun but also the moon at this time of equinox.

I found a place among the apple trees in the orchard to sit, smelling the apple smells in the air and sitting on the grass, feeling the air around me and just letting my thoughts drift for a while.

Again I was pulled to walk, so leaving through the orchard gate I walked along the trackway, this was one of the levels of the labyrinth, to find myself on the level below the eggstone, the entrance to the inside of the labyrinth. Not wanting to climb the short steep way to the eggstone itself because I always find that last little bit of the climb to the eggstone challenging, not liking heights, or rather slopes I rarely go and sit there.

    I stood looking around. It took me a moment realise this was the place where I had taken part in a ceremony a few years ago. It looked so different now, so many nettles around and the space looked smaller, but the more I looked I realised that yes, this was the place.

Looking around I could see the places in the distant landscape just as I remembered them from that ceremony. Standing looking it seemed to go cold, the sun went briefly behind a cloud and the wind became a bit cooler, so I walked away, back the way I had come. I had only got a short way when I sensed something was not quite right.
Need I go back to the place where I had just been?

I started to walk slowly back but got the message that no, going back wasn't the answer but what should I do?

I wasn't sure so just stood there looking around me, trying to sense feelings. I started to walk a bit nearer again to the place below the eggstone but got such a strong message of no, going back wasn't right.

So I stood again and looked at the place where I had just been.

There was something I needed to do and I now knew what it was.

A part of letting go of the past, of something I had been involved with here. It came to me what I needed to do and it is something between only me and that moment and not something I can share through words. All I will say is I did what I needed to do and when I had done so, I sensed lightness and a closure like a door being shut.

I had intended to connect more with Gwyn here but it turned into cutting ties and maybe closing doors but moving forward in different ways!

Chapter 5

Glastonbury Tor

Glastonbury Tor

Over the next few weeks I found myself walking on Glastonbury Tor around three or four times a week. Part of this was completing the walks and recording them, plus taking photographs for my Walking book, but part of this was also my exploration of who Gwyn ap Nudd was. It was as if I was being 'called by him' to walk the land of the Isle. I walked in all weathers, autumn sunshine, warmth and cold, lashing rain and drizzle and only very occasionally floating mist.

Not much more was coming to me about Gwyn as I walked, nothing more had emerged in my thoughts apart from those first few images and ideas when I had walked on the hill.

Maybe I was trying too hard?

I had read a bit about him, the legends telling how he lived under Glastonbury Tor, how he emerged at Samhain riding with the Wild Hunt across the land, riding with his warriors and hounds. How he re-entered his underground home each Beltane before emerging again the following Samhain. That he was also the King of the Fae, the folk who live under the hill with him and if you entered his realm you need not eat or drink anything offered or you would not be able to leave. I read more legends about him but I will leave those for you to find.

I would walk not only up to the top of Glastonbury Tor, sometimes sitting and leaning against the tower looking at the views of countryside all around but also sometimes just walking on the lower levels of this magical hill, drawn to walk on, and around, sitting, walking, taking photographs, musing.

Glastonbury Tor is a magical place, sometimes the steps seem really steep and it seems hard to get to the top and at other times it seems easy.

I have been up to the top when it is so busy with people that it's hard to move around and at other times only a few people have been there, very rarely have I been alone there.

On one occasion the National Trust were doing erosion repairs on the very top and had a helicopter from the nearby naval base taking erosion control supplies to the top, the helicopter blades looking as if they would at any point knock the tower over, though it was an illusion of view from where I stood and they weren't that close.

People visit this magical hill from all over the world, the views are magnificent and change each time I visit. It can be so atmospheric in the rain and mist, I had climbed to the top of the hill on a very rainy day and while standing looking at the hazy view, the rain sweeping across the land, the mist descended for a short while completely blocking out any view of the land below, all I could see was the place where I stood. Then the mist cleared again and the view was once again seen. I had, along with the others there that day, been in the cloud for a short while.

Walking up Glastonbury Tor via the concrete footpath and steps is easy for me if I go up from the Chalice Well side via the Fairfield but hard for me if I go up the steps from the Moneybox field side. I rarely go up Moneybox field side, I find the footpath in parts looks as if it is on a steep sideways slope and that challenges me. I feel as if I am going to 'fall off' and become very frightened, so for that reason I always go up the Chalice well side, though a longer way to walk the hill is slightly flatter on either side of the path.

But as challenges go what did I find, yes, you've guessed it, I found myself quite a few times walking up the steps via the Moneybox field side, sometimes terrified but always wondering to myself 'why am I doing this?'.

I found myself calling to Gwyn to help me overcome my fear, to help me get to the top of the hill. After all I didn't have the option of going back down this way, going up was bad, going down was impossible for me. So I called to Gwyn and I would get a sense of him being there with me, helping me get past the 'very scary for me' part of the path, not looking around as I climbed but just looking at each step I had to take to get me to the top. Why, oh why, did I do this?

Then I would get to the top of the hill, breathe out a huge sigh of relief and have a sense of achievement that I had done it. That is why I did it!

I would then spend time sitting, walking around the top of the hill, feeling the place, and seeing the views stretching into the distance all around. Sometimes I would stay awhile but others only a short time before going down the longer way!

I was also being challenged on these walks in another way. I am not a 'natural person' with animals, past experiences of being bitten by dogs and not liking the size of cows or horses unless they were on the other side of a fence or hedge, made me a nervous person around these animals. Strangely sheep don't bother me at all and I can quite happily walk among and through a field or fields of sheep. So I was quite surprised to find myself being 'challenged' by animals on some of my walks and the help I was offered.

For instance on one walk the footpath went through a field for which I had to climb over a stile to get in and out the other side of the field. However, there were two horses in the field and I stood on 'my side' of the fence not knowing what to do. It was a long way to walk back the way I had come, the walk having taken me down from the Tor, past Gog and Magog the two ancient oak trees, and now through fields and eventually back into town. So you can see I was hesitant in turning round and re-climbing the fields back towards the Tor, but equally I didn't want to walk through the field with the horses in it! What to do? Then a man arrived to feed the horses, I watched him as he went towards them and when he was with them; I climbed over the stile and walked very quickly over the field and out the other side. I said 'Hello' to him when I was in the safety of 'my other side of the field' again and told him I was frightened of horses. He told me the horses were very gentle and would let schoolchildren and visitors to the farm come and pat them and would I like to do that. I thanked him but said not at this time, for me it was a challenge too far and continued on my walk.

The next time I faced animals it was dogs, now I don't like dogs, having been bitten several times when I was a child and I know they sense my nervousness. I was sitting on the bench near to the bottom of the Tor, hardly anyone else was around, when I saw a man walking up the path with what looked like several wolves but were actually dogs. / I can't quite remember how many there were, three maybe but they were off lead. I sat there so frightened, not knowing what to do, so didn't do anything. I found when they got closer that they just walked past me. The man said 'Hello' to me and I said the same back and also said how dogs made me nervous. He, like the man with the horses, invited me to meet the dogs but again I declined, again it was a fear too far.

On the third occasion I was walking from Bushy Coombe and intended to go across the field and onto the country road to go to the Tor. When I got to the field gate though, I saw cows grazing in the field. They hadn't been there the day before and I didn't know what to do, they looked huge and were grazing right in the way of the footpath. I stood there thinking 'the field is big, why do they have to graze right by the footpath?' I didn't know what to do, again as on my other walks, I didn't want to walk back the way I had come, so I waited for someone else to come along on the footpath. I thought I could ask if I would be able to walk across the field with them. and who should be the first person to come along the footpath, yes you've guessed it! A man with a dog! After explaining to him my fear he very kindly let me walk across the field with him and I continued my walk to the Tor.

I was being challenged but I was also being offered help! I am and always will be frightened and nervous around animals and I know I was offered a chance to start to face these fears I also knew I wasn't at a point to do that. They were a step too far for me.

Was this Gwyn ap Nudd challenging me?

What do you think?

Chapter 6

Challenges

Challenges

I was involved at that time in the planning for the Glastonbury Dragons Celebrations and the very first Samhain Wild Hunt. My partner, Steve had made and created the two Glastonbury Red and White Dragons which had appeared for the very first time in May at the Beltane event. This time for Samhain he had the idea to create a throne for Gwyn Ap Nudd, a throne that would carry Gwyn from the market cross area of town up onto the Fairfield on the lower slopes of Glastonbury Tor. The throne was built in our garden before being painted; I saw it emerging from those very first ideas on paper, to the first bits of wood being put together and then the actual throne completed. It was made so Gwyn could sit in it and be carried; long handles from the chair/throne part enabled it to be picked up and carried by up to eight people.

A person had been chosen to be Gwyn; or I rather think Gwyn chose him than the other way around. Gwyn had not been represented in this way as a physical person at all in the town before. Despite all the myths and legends this would be the first time that he was emerging and being honored in this way. The man chosen to be Gwyn ap Nudd was asked to create his own mask and this he did, spending time creating, painting and putting energy into it. I was at that time the photographer for the Dragon events; I would take photos on the day, edit them and then share them as a record of the event.

The day of Samhain came, so off I went to take the photographs of the event. Now I know the person who was 'being Gwyn', not very well but I knew what he looked like and to say 'hello' to him along with his family. So I knew who I was looking for to take the photographs of and what his voice sounded like, or that's what I thought!

I walked into the town, seeing so many people, taking photographs of all and everything, capturing the essence of the day. People were dressed in blacks and furs and all sorts of clothes and costumes, horned headdresses, hats and more.

I was fascinated while taking the photographs then I came across Gwyn. I could see him standing a short way away from me, so I went closer to capture him in image. He looked so impossibly tall, as if he was stretching to the sky. He spoke and said 'hello' to me in a voice I didn't recognise at all. I was now nervous; standing trying to take some photographs of this 'presence', for it was formidable and powerful. A tall man covered in furs and layers, he wore a mask of blues and blacks, swirls, and antler shapes. Because of the mask I couldn't see his eyes! I took some photographs and then moved among the crowd to take more, leaving Gwyn standing there.

Then it was time for Gwyn to be carried from town up to the Fairfield on the lower slopes of Glastonbury Tor. With horns blowing the procession set off, carrying Gwyn in his throne were his tribe. Now this hadn't been planned when the event planning was taking place but something that just happened on the day. A tribe of people came along with Gwyn, people who he knew, they were all dressed in furs or cloaks and some with horns and they carried him along to the Fairfield. They really did look so tribal and timeless carrying him along. Arriving at the Fairfield the throne was placed facing towards the town with Glastonbury Tor behind and when everyone was gathered the ceremony started. The day was now growing dusk and in the growing twilight Gwyn stood, arms held high, his voice carrying in the air announcing his re-emergence and return!

Gwyn in his physical presence had announced his return, the first time he had done so in this way on Glastonbury Tor. I found it a very mixed and powerful time. The ceremony taking place in late afternoon, Glastonbury Tor behind me, I watched and took photographs with the lights of the land below gradually flickering on and becoming brighter as the day became darker and early evening fell.

Again I found myself standing near to Gwyn but this time I could see his eyes, and what I saw surprised me. I had expected him to have hard looking eyes, the eyes of a warrior, showing no emotion or feeling. What I saw were the eyes of a warrior but with kindness inside, there was warmth there. Surrounded by his tribe he looked so at home on the slopes of Glastonbury Tor. I stood for a while thinking, wondering why I was surprised that Gwyn wasn't what I had expected him to be, after all Pan wasn't what I expected him to be either! In the now dark evening I made my way home, knowing I had a lot of photographs to edit, walking along the pathways others around me, all returning to the town.

Did I think that was it?

That he had emerged and I need do no more?

Well yes I did but no he didn't!

I found my journey with Gwyn wasn't over yet. He had called me to walk on his realm, on the hill, the footpaths and lanes around the Tor leading up to his re-emergence. While I walked, as often happens, words whispered on the breeze and I wrote them down.

It is in the wild places where I roam
Between the veils that's where you will find my home
Through the worlds when the veils are thin
If I emerge will you let me in?
If I beckon will you come stand by me?
Roaming the land, wild and free

Travel through the veils
When the mists are thin
Open up your eyes
Let the journey begin

In the days and weeks that followed I found myself still walking around and on Glastonbury Tor, still being pulled to walk on the magical hill. Recording my walks and taking photographs, intending some of them to be used for my books and some for the Gwyn exhibition that my friend and I had planned.

Gwyn and his Wild Hunt were now roaming the land; the King of the Fae had left his home under Glastonbury Tor and was once again wild and free.

As I walk on your realm on Glastonbury Tor
I know you have emerged once again
Through the opened door
When the veils were thin
We helped open the door
So you could be free
On your land once more

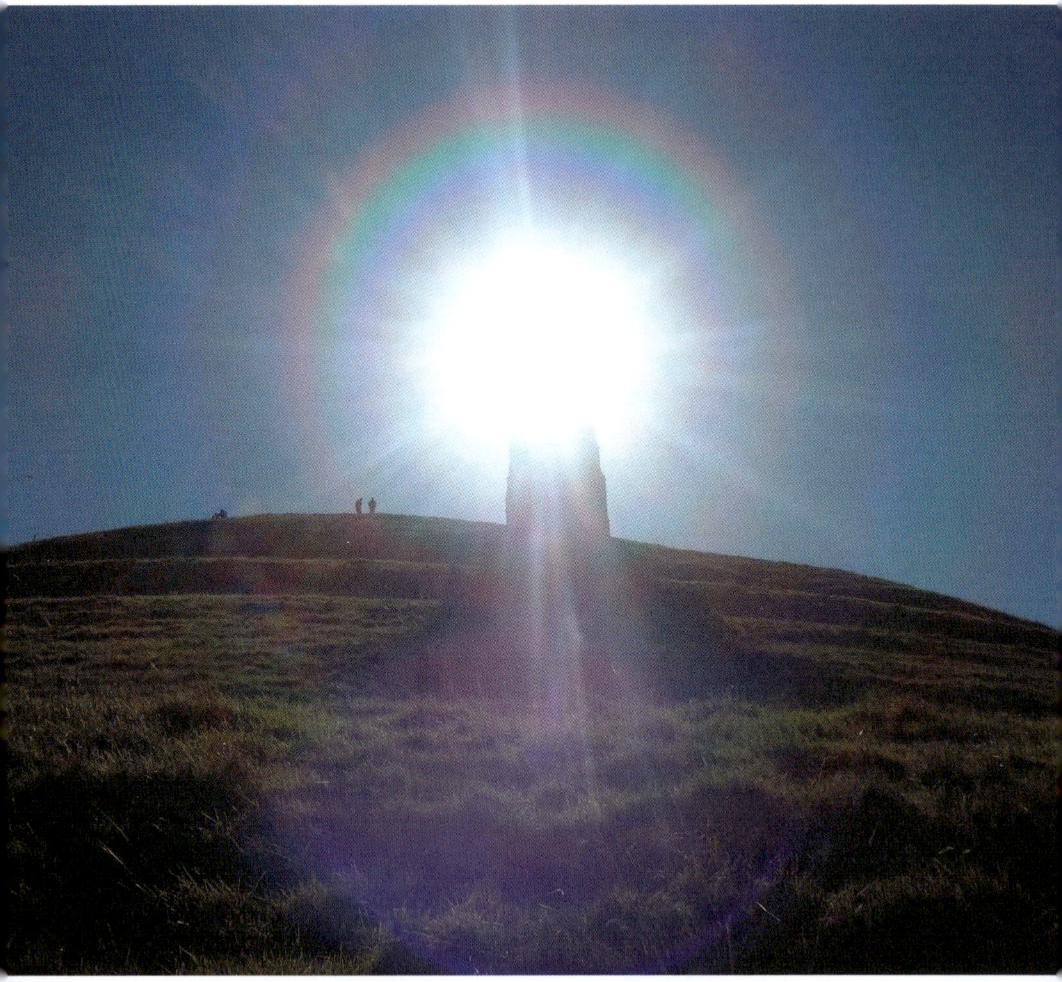

I carried on being drawn to walk the lanes and land on and around Glastonbury Tor, all the while still writing and producing my books. I had released my book The Woodland and the Fae in spring 2016. This book is a combination of full colour collage images, created from my original photographs and verse. It's really about Pan and my journey with him, my discovery of the woodland and of the male. How I had decided to let the male into my life again, after previously having difficult experiences with the male throughout my life.

I was, as said before, I am comfortable with Pan, but Gwyn, not yet.

Taking photographs I had images that I wanted to develop, to show what I was seeing but I wasn't sure how to do that. I had words but I wasn't sure what to do with them. With my friend a very talented and inspirational artist we planned to do an exhibition together and although she doesn't live in town we decided to hold an exhibition in Glastonbury. I priced up some spaces to find most were beyond our budget but we both felt that an exhibition was needed to show and honour the God.

We had planned to exhibit in 2017 around Samhain time but Gwyn had other ideas. Since he had 'emerged' at Samhain he had taken me on quite a journey of discovery and challenges. Some I don't choose to share for very personal and deep reasons but one of those challenges I can share because it is a part of this journey which I am sharing in this book. I was still involved with the Dragons planning organisation but I had been getting the feeling that I wanted to leave. I felt that I had done all I needed to do and it was time to move on but I also had a strong sense that I needed to stay until Gwyn 'went back' into his home under the Tor at Beltane. So despite feeling that I should leave I stayed, and in hindsight this was the wrong choice!

The Dragons Beltane event took place and once again I found myself standing on the Fairfield with Glastonbury Tor behind me and the town and land before me but this time it was May and the land was warming and beginning to stir. Gwyn was returning and would go into his home under the Tor for the next 6 months. The ceremony took place, I can't remember much of it now but I do remember after it finished standing on the Fairfield, looking up towards the top of the Tor, seeing the very top of the tower on the horizon. I just stood looking, standing so still, just feeling, then I felt such an enormous sense of relief and lightness, It felt as if I had been holding a breath and let it go, as if the sun had just emerged again from the mist. What I didn't know until later that day, was the man who had held Gwyn and his energies for the past 6 months had gone with a small group of people to the top of the Tor and released back privately into the Tor, the energy he had held. It turned out it was the same time as I had the feeling of release and lightness while I stood on the Fairfield.

I returned home and for a week or so carried on with projects I was working on, walking, and photographing, typing and editing, for other ideas I had.

Then, just after May, Gwyn blew apart our exhibition plans; he blew apart my connection to being part of the planning group and photographer for the Glastonbury Dragons. He certainly gave me a huge challenge and made me look very deeply into myself and how I appeared to others.

I had been involved with a group in Glastonbury before. A large group I was heavily involved with and which had become a huge part of my life when I first moved. Then after being a part of this group for several years, the 'rose tinted glasses' gradually faded and I saw the reality. I saw how it really was and I saw the injustice of what was happening.

I spoke out and walked away.

Why?

Because while I could accept a lot of things I could not accept the injustice I was seeing happening and the way people were being treated.

What followed at that time was a very difficult and challenging journey of questioning and looking at the things I did, looking at my creativity and how to rebuild my income and the way I showed myself. But never once did I waver in my connection to Goddess, I questioned myself and knew that I had dedicated to her and I would and always will be her Priestess, whether visible to others or not. I now knew I had to find my own way.

One of my questions to myself was - how do I see Goddess?

I see Goddess in the land, I feel her when I walk, the ground beneath my feet, the shape of the land, the hills, and valleys. I feel her in the elements as I walk, the air around me, the water of the rain touching me, the heat of the sun on me, the soft earth beneath me. These feelings change with the seasons and weather within the seasons but the connection is still there, whether the heat of the summer sun or the cold of the winter wind, the dry earth, which is hard in summer, or the wet muddy, soft earth in winter. That is part of her beauty, her constantly changing but seemingly remaining the same.

It took me three years after walking away to rebuild my life, to look at what Goddess meant to me, to try and earn an income while hiding away.

I found true, new friends and a whole new world opened up for me, a different layer of the town where I lived showed itself to me as well. What I also found, with the support of my partner and the path we walked together was duality. We walk not behind or in front of each other but alongside, we honour the Goddess and the God. For it was at this time that I also discovered Pan and the story already told in this book earlier on.

Even so through this part of the journey, it still didn't change the fact that I did not want to be 'seen'. I had sort of emerged slightly in my involvement with the Dragons, with wanting to help the whole community of the town where I lived, but once again I was being challenged though this time someone else had triggered that change................

The God, not the Goddess was challenging me this time!

Chapter 7

Looking and Questioning

Looking and questioning

I felt now that I was in a similar place to the one three years earlier and didn't know what to do. I wanted to hide, I wanted to run, I didn't want my partner with me, not because I didn't love him deeply but because I didn't feel I was worth it. He had other ideas though and he didn't go away. I was so hurt emotionally, I am not perfect, I have never claimed to be and never will be but sometimes the action of others causes hurt and pain beyond our control.

So I asked myself,

'What didn't I learn last time?'

'What do I need to see now?'

Again I was seeing similar happenings in my relationships with people I thought I knew, people I thought I could trust emerging for what they were, the reality and not the illusion. I looked deeply inside myself, at how I was seen, how I came across to others. I understood that being 'Northern', I could come across as being 'abrupt'.
(I am actually originally from Derbyshire, which is technically the Midlands, but try telling Southerners that. And I mean no disrespect to anyone here, I like both Northern and Southern people)
What's the difference between Northern and Southern you ask?
In my experience Northerners just 'say it as it is' where Southerners 'go round the houses before getting to the point'. Neither way is right or wrong but I have never gone the long route in my speech and always just 'said it as it is', getting me into trouble sometimes I must admit. I started to adjust or soften how I said things. I also realised that the last time I had been in this kind of situation I had spoken out the once but remained silent after that. That has been one of the hardest things I have ever done. Now though, I realised that I didn't want to remain silent this time, so I spoke to some people and

voiced my thoughts. That's all I needed to do, nothing more. Then I wanted to run away and hide again and that's what I did. Not run away, that was impossible at the time with no money to do that but I did hide by not seeing people and going into the fields walking rather than go into town much.

Who am I
Am I sure that I can fly
When people look at me
What do they see
Insignificant me
Do they only see the parts I want to show
What do they know

Why do I care not to show
Who I am, what I see
Why are they so dismissive of me
Do they know more than I
Can they too soar through the sky
Can they touch lands only some see
Connect with the world tree

Can they go deep inside
Journey through fear and the deep intense sea
Touch the beings only some see
Am I such an insignificant me
Flying and riding the deep intense sea
Through the world tree

As I journey inside to the places I hide
To the power within me
Do I then care to let all see
Or just the ones who are like me

I didn't want to carry on planning the exhibition at all but my friend talked to me on the phone. She told me we needed to do this, that although it wasn't working yet it would do, that she wouldn't let me give up. But would I?

I was still walking around Glastonbury Tor. We didn't have a car at this point and unless I walked I couldn't get anywhere. Buses weren't an option as we didn't have a lot of money either, so I felt restricted.

I walked on the lanes and footpaths around the town and the Tor enjoying the change of season and weather.

I was drawn quite a lot at this time to sit in the Avalon Orchard on the lower slopes of the Tor. I would sit on the ground, my little waterproof mat beneath me, smelling the smells of apples growing and seeing the land stretching beyond the apple trees. The orchard is on a slope and sitting near the top you can see the view beyond through the apple trees to the distant hills.

I was sitting there one day with my partner; it was springtime and the sheep from Moneybox field started to come through the gate at the bottom of the orchard with their new born lambs. We watched the Mummy sheep bleating and calling when they realised their lambs weren't right behind them and then the lambs bleating and calling when they found their Mummies. The sheep came into the bottom of the orchard and wandered around, some going off into the next field but some sitting and relaxing, munching the grass.

It was an enchanting experience to watch but also puzzled me. I originally come from Derbyshire where there are so many sheep that they become the norm rather than a novelty, so why was I now so fascinated by these sheep?

It was then while watching the sheep and talking to my partner that the idea of stories came to me, stories that would become 'The Lambs of Avalon'. Children's stories that would combine my love of the land with the Arthurian myths and legends and of course Gwyn! By featuring lambs rather than people I could use far more imagination in the tales; after all I haven't heard lambs talk!

The tales feature two main characters, lambs called Tristan and Alfred who live in the field by a strange hill, a hill known as Glastonbury Tor. Their best friends are Blodeuwedd and Morgana, two other lambs and they are guided on adventures by a bird called Merlin. In the very first tale they meet Gwyn ap Nudd and through this tale I give a glimpse of how I found his energy and his emergence, a mixture of fascination, fear, and challenge.

An extract from 'The Lambs of Avalon, The Adventures of Tristan and Alfred' where they meet Gwyn ap Nudd.

'Tristan and Alfred sat as Merlin had asked, crouching down in the grass by the old molehill. They watched the strange egg stone, the noises getting louder now and then all of a sudden the large egg stone slid to the side. The light became brighter and they could see that the egg stone was actually a doorway, which had been slid aside opening up the hill itself.

They could hear another noise now and tried to crouch down even more into the earth, hoping their white wooly coats could not be seen. They could feel hoof beats in the earth where they were, the feeling getting stronger and stronger, while the noise became louder and louder.

Something was coming, they knew that now, but what was coming they did not know.

Merlin shushed them to help calm them and keep their fears away while the noise got even louder. Tristan and Alfred shook with fear so strong a feeling they couldn't move anyway.

Just as they thought they may try to run away they saw what was making the noise. It was a group of horses, hooves hammering the ground as they rode up the hill, white light surrounding all of them, like a hazy mist. They were being guided by the light from the open egg stone doorway.

They could see figures on the horses; the main figure had antlers full of leaves, bracken and grass tangled within them.

As he got nearer they could see the markings on his face, black, purple and blue swirls in some kind of strange pattern. His hair was dark black with the hint of a beard. He wore furs of brown and black leather trousers, with boots to match, his feet in stirrups of gold.

The horses slowed as they came nearer to the egg stone doorway. Just at that moment a moonlit beam shone onto the main figure, highlighting his eyes. Eyes so soft and gentle, full of kindness and colours of the night, blacks and browns with a hint of the green of earth, but also eyes that could be stern and hard if need be.

The moment went. The riders sped up and rode straight into the passage behind the open doorway. When the last of the riders had entered, the doorway slid shut again.'

I was also at this time creating another walking book and writing the Lambs tales when my friend and I had the chance to book some exhibition space. She was in town at a conference and we called into the Galleries to find they had a slot free the following year, so we booked it.

Gwyn really did want this exhibition to go ahead!

But I was still hiding, not wanting to be seen, after all who was I?

What am I
Who am I
The person inside, who am I
Witch, Enchantress, Sorceress, lover
Who am I
How do I fly
Lady of the land, is that I
Who am I
Who is it within me, how do I fly
Am I the Witch who casts the spell
Am I the Enchantress who conjures the wind
Am I the Sorceress who hears all sing
Who's lover am I
Who am I
When I walk on the land,
my feet on the earth
Who's land is it
What is my worth

Chapter 8

Realisation

Realisation

I was learning in knowledge and through the people I met. Spending time walking the land I started to look again at me. I had no confidence in myself, in what I knew and it didn't help and still doesn't that I am a very secretive, private person. I find it hard to open up to people I don't know and even to those who I do know. So I would sit, muse, write and meditate, gradually becoming stronger in who I was but still hiding, still not emerging again. Like Gwyn I hid in the inner world, after all he has two worlds, inner and outer. I could definitely feel that he had gone back to his home inside Glastonbury Tor in the same way that I could feel when he was roaming the land on his emergence.

I was nervous of me; I was nervous of Gwyn; he had challenged me so much that I was wary of him. Did I really want to do an exhibition; did I really want to share my journey of discovery of him?

After all I had put myself 'up there' twice now with different groups and had been challenged both times, did I now want to do this again with an exhibition?

Don't get me wrong, I am not self-centred; I don't spend hours and hours looking inside and working out who I am, this only reflects a short part of my day. I have done the 'normal' things, brought up a family, seen my adult children fly the nest and become families themselves, gone through deep loss and changed lifestyles and counties. I have realised that I am an artist - a writer, a poet, a photographer and put my time into that. All this takes a huge amount of time and if I wasn't writing and creating my books and photographs I wouldn't have the time to walk and explore the land as part of these, this all this comes with a lot of pressure as well, because there is no guaranteed income and we live hand to mouth.

I also realised what I do, being an artist, is part of my sensitivity, my creativity and as all artists will tell you, in whatever form they create and produce, you are 'putting yourself up there'. Getting criticised for doing something while working say in an office may hurt but it's not personal, not usually anyway, getting criticised for your own creativity hurts and feels personal and goes more deeply. But it's the nature of the game, not everyone will love what an artist does and I am realistic enough to understand that. I have my favourite artists and writers like anyone else but even within those there may be pieces or books that I am not so keen on, it's such a variable dance to dance!

Gwyn had emerged again at Samhain. This time I didn't take part in the event or be there. I did however, go and walk on the Tor, standing looking for a while down towards the Fairfield, seeing the people gather once again for his return to the land, for his chase with the wild hunt.

A different person was representing Gwyn this time, I didn't know who he was but once again he had been carried in the throne from the Market Cross to the field beneath the Tor. I didn't stay long but also this time I didn't get the intense feeling of energy being released, even though I felt he had emerged again it was more subtle this time.

I was nervous about his energy being released again and tried to put him to the back of my mind, however, he hovered there, just out of sight.

Half the year passed again and once again at Beltane he returned to his home under the Tor and I had put the exhibition to the back of my mind.

I have highs and lows, my highs are high and my lows very deep, I didn't want to journey with Gwyn, to go into his energies, so I kept myself busy. But I also suffer from stress and it can be very intense, I became very stressed and couldn't settle. We still didn't have a car at that time, we had been without one for nearly two years. So we could only occasionally 'escape from the Isle' when a friend lent us a car, I felt as if I was on some kind of retreat, being held on the Isle! I created and worked and kept busy but meanwhile those images of Gwyn were resurfacing, wanting to be seen but not only images, the story of how I experienced finding him.

How would I show him for the exhibition, after all my skill isn't in drawing, I am not an artist in that way. My skill is in words and how I see things through photography. I had the idea for a very short while of photographing a man dressed as Gwyn with horns and mask and then creating collage images from those photographs. But I never got round to getting someone to pose and taking those photographs. Gwyn to me was more than just that image but how would I show him, after all my original idea for the landscape photographs was to use them as background images.

Then I realised that Gwyn was the land, both inside and out, just like the Goddess, who for me has many aspects, he is one of the aspects of the God. Like my emotions and feelings, my questioning and doubt, my confidence and what I show to others, he is the same. He hides for half the year and is visible for half the year. Like the inner and outer they are both aspects of the same. Like the different faces I show to the world, to others, he shows different faces to whoever he meets.

You may see and experience a different Gwyn to me.

But the Gwyn I see is in the land I walk and the words that come to me and I realised that was what I needed to show for the exhibition, the land rather than the person. Though he still wanted his story told of how I discovered him!

So this is my story, you have read my words.

Yours will be different; it will be your story.

If he calls, you have a choice, or do you?

Go journey to meet him, experience him, go see what he shows to you.

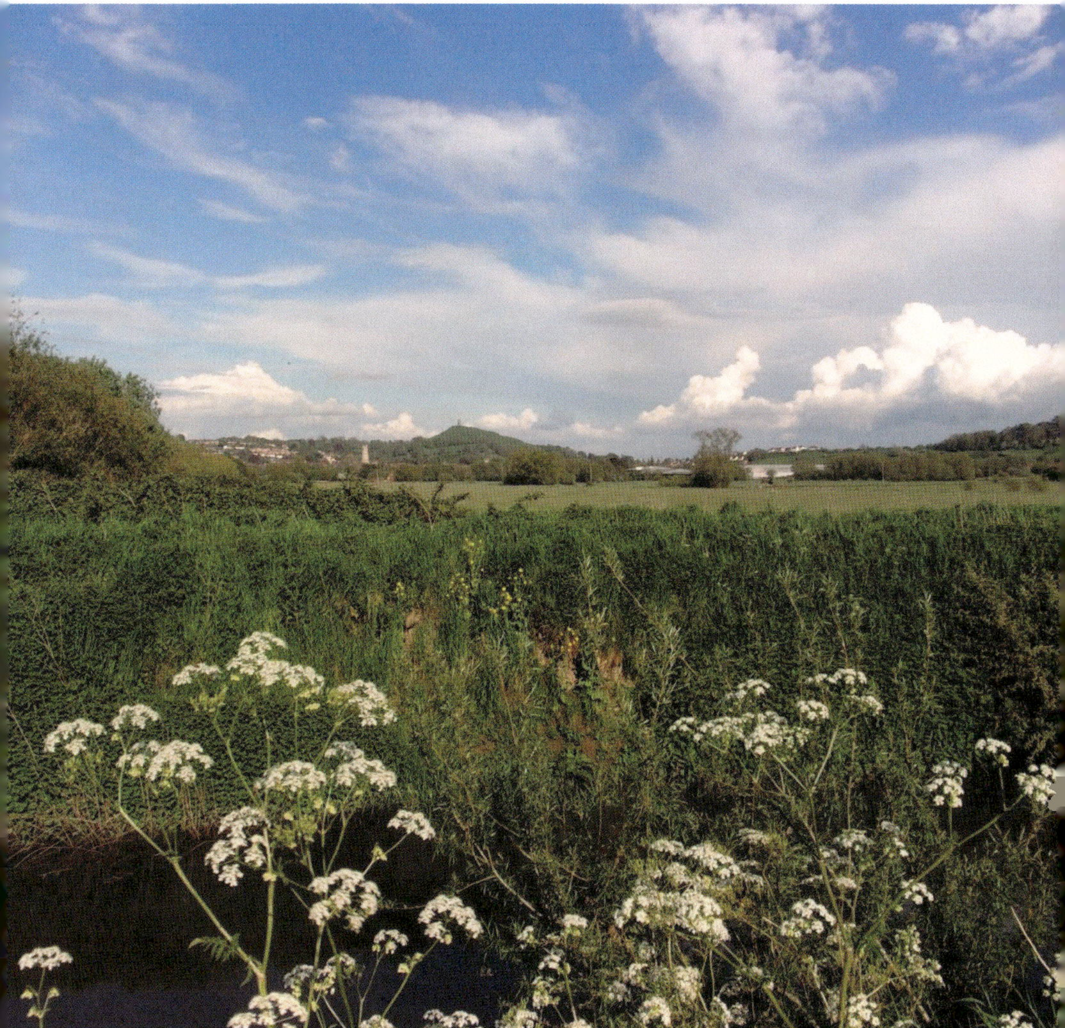

*Wisdom isn't something learnt
But something inside
In a place you can't always find
It can be hidden so deep
In the bottom of a pool
Or in the deepest cave
In the middle of nowhere
Floating thoughts on the air
If you find your wisdom
For some never do
The wisdom is yours, only for you
What you do then
Is up to you*

Chapter 9

Gwyn ap Nudd in image and verse

Gwyn ap Nudd in image and verse

Come enter the other realms with me

Time stands still
As I sit on the hill
The hill of mystery and time
A place of the otherworld still

It is in the wild places where I roam
Between the veils.........
that's where you will find my home
Through the worlds when the veils are thin
If I emerge, will you let me in?
If I beckon will you come stand by me?
Roaming the land wild and free

This is my realm; can you hear me call?
To remember the land
As moonbeam light, guides the way
Will you journey with me, will you see?

Will you help me emerge
Step onto the land where myth and magick merge
As the trees shed their leaves for all to see
I come from my island home to reclaim my majesty

Follow the November sun
In the pale blue sky
To find the spark of the moon
Where you will hear my cry

Follow the November sun
In the pale blue sky
To the spark of the moon
Where you will hear my cry

Travel through the veils
When the mists are thin
Open up your eyes
Let the journey begin

When the confetti of leaves falls on the breeze
Showing the key to the door that's opened once more
When the land is covered in leaves of all shades
and the pathways are covered making it hard to see
the way to tread unless you know the way

For the pathways are secret, unless you know what to say
So when you feel the leaves blowing against you skin
They are showing you where to begin
Whisper he words you need me to hear
Then the land you need to see will become clear

This book is about my journey discovering Gwyn, through the Goddess and the God, through the land and seasons, the inner and outer worlds. This is my journey with him while walking and exploring The Isle of Avalon - Glastonbury Tor, the sacred and magical hill.

If you choose to hear his call and journey with him, your journey will be yours alone.

Are you ready?

The Isle of Avalon - Glastonbury Tor
Looking from Wearyall Hill

The following pages are for your own notes and thoughts

Vanda Lloyd's other books and photography can be found on: -

Website: https://lloydbux.wixsite.com/vanda-lloyd

Facebook page – Avalon Dreaming, Glastonbury

© Words and photography Vanda Lloyd – October 2018